AF270754

GOD *is*
BIGGER
than your
GRIEF

**FRESH
WATER
PRESS**

Grover, Missouri

Fresh Water Press
P.O. Box 18
Grover, MO 63040
www.Godisbiggerthan.com

Although the author and publisher have made every effort to ensure the accuracy and completeness of information contained in this book, we assume no responsibility for errors, inaccuracies, omissions or any inconsistency herein. Any slights of people, places or organizations are unintentional.

First printing 2008

ISBN 978-0-9801591-2-7

ATTENTION HOSPICE AND
BEREAVEMENT ORGANIZATIONS:
Quantity discounts are available on bulk purchases of this book for educational or gift purposes. Special books or book excerpts can also be created to fit specific needs.
For information, please contact:
Fresh Water Press
P.O. Box 18
Grover, MO 63040
www.Godisbiggerthan.com

To

Granny Liz

who attempted to teach me how to
buy a proper frock,
set a proper table
and
sit like a proper lady

all the while displaying

the **power** of **loyalty**,
the **value** of **family** and **friends**
and
the **wisdom** and **faith** of a

True Believer

Contents

Chapter One

Will I See Them Again?

He's waiting
on the **hearts**
of those who
push Him away.

Listening for Doorbells

$\mathcal{N}$o one likes to talk about death. My grandmother used to say that death isn't proper dinner conversation. But death is hard to talk about anywhere and anytime. Why? Because there is no amount of problem solving, strategizing or analyzing that can eliminate it. Seat belts, bicycle helmets and yearly physicals are attempts to keep our bodies going, but, eventually, this life and this body, as we know it, dies.

When death takes someone you loved, whom you know loved Jesus, friends tell you, "He is in a better place." "He is finally not suffering."

You respond, "I know."

But then someone says, "You'll be with him again in heaven. This is just a temporary separation."

That is the promise you want to believe with all heart. *"Will I? Will I see him again? Is this thing called death really temporary?"* To wake each morning knowing that you will be reunited with your loved one in heaven would mean so much. Yet every logical conclusion is that death is final, even though your faith tells you Jesus conquered death. If that's true, if Jesus *did* conquer death, why do people still die?

People were not supposed to die. That's a hard truth to grasp when death is such a prominent part of living on earth today, but it's true. When God made Adam, the plan was for God to dwell among His people, forever. For Adam, dwelling with God meant long strolls through the garden in the cool of the evening.

Now, try to remember, Adam was strolling with

the Lord God Almighty, who was powerful enough to create the heavens and the earth with just a word. Just a word! He spoke and there were oceans and continents and stars and all the stuff that goes with them. Let's face it. That's a lot of power! (After all, I get nervous just standing next to my husband's boss, who is powerful enough to make paying bills difficult.) I can't even imagine strolling with God!

Why didn't Adam spontaneously combust from being within a hundred miles of that type of power? Why? The answer is — Adam was perfect! To hang out with God, you have to be completely perfect and clean.

Of course, all of that changed when Adam and his girl, Eve, ate the forbidden fruit. Bottom line: they disobeyed God. Suddenly, death and sin came to mankind. From that point on, God's precious children were no longer clean and perfect enough to dwell with God.

God hated this! Getting us all back together with Him became His total purpose. All God needed to make His children clean again was someone to offer himself as a pure and perfect sacrifice. The big problem was, since the whole eating-the-forbidden-fruit thing, no one on earth was perfect. That's why God sent His Son, Jesus. Jesus lived a sin-free life: He was pure.

Jesus didn't have to die so He could be pure enough to dwell with God. But He chose to die on the cross in our place, so *we* can dwell with God for all eternity. When Jesus rose from the grave, He was victorious over death! Hebrews 2:9 tells us that Jesus "... suffered death, so that by the grace of God He might taste death for everyone."

If that is so—if Jesus conquered death on the cross—why are people still dying? Why can't all believers just stroll with God through His heavenly gardens *now* and call off living on earth? Good question. You see, the battle is won and death is conquered; now Jesus is just waiting for the victory party.

In 2001, several significant events coincided in my life: My husband began a new job, we moved from the Midwest to Southern California and our youngest child entered first grade. So here I was, with an over-worked husband, no friends and an empty house. To battle immense feelings of loneliness, there was only one thing to do—have a party. In hindsight, it seems a little bizarre, but at the time it seemed to make sense.

My previous party planning experience revolved around kindergarteners and fast food restaurants. But you can't let a little thing like not knowing what you're doing slow you down. Although I believed real Mexican food came from Taco Bell, I thought I knew enough to throw a real Mexican fiesta!

For months I tested new recipes, found tablecloths on sale, bought serving dishes, rented chafing dishes, ordered homemade tamales and, of course, hunted for something to wear. Just when I thought the work was all done, I'd think of something else to do.

Finally, the day of the party arrived. The rental guys are gone, the kids are at the sitter's, the stereo is cranked, the candles are lit, the food is ready and

"I'm in the

there I sit. All the work is behind me. There's nothing left to do but enjoy the evening, but it's not time yet. I'm in the waiting zone, watching the door and desperately listening for the doorbell to ring and my first guest to walk through the door.

Jesus is in the waiting zone too. He has completely defeated sin and death and is waiting for His victory party to begin. God will one day tell Jesus to fetch His guests and escort them through the doors of heaven. Imagine standing in the throne room of heaven, with all the believers since the beginning of time, including your saved loved one!

Being reunited has never tasted so sweet. You're dressed in not just new clothes, but in a whole new body. The angels are singing, the band is rockin' and don't even get me going on the menu! Then you see God face-to-face! Really! The blood of Christ on the cross has washed you and your loved one so pure that you will be made perfect in God's sight. That means you get to move in and live with God!

Revelation 21 gives us a glimmer of how sweet

waiting zone,

this will be: "Now the dwelling of God is with men, and He will live with them. They will be His people, and God Himself will be with them and be their God. He will wipe every tear from their eyes. There will be no more death or mourning or crying or pain, for the old order of things has passed away" (Revelation 21:3-4).

Try to fathom: no more death, mourning, crying or pain. Picture a gentle hand, wiping away your last tear. This is dwelling with God.

Can you hardly wait? Neither can I!

Then why is Jesus waiting? He's waiting on the one thing He hasn't conquered yet: the hearts of those who push Him away. God is not willing to start the party until every person who belongs there accepts His invitation. Think of someone you know who does not believe in Jesus. God is waiting on that person, and countless others, whom He hungers to save.

If only there was some way to dwell with God now—to know that God is with your every breath,

...watching the door

every thought and every hope. Here's the really amazing thing: God has placed a drop of Himself in each believer. As believers, we dwell with God each moment of our days, because the Holy Spirit is living within us. You are not alone!

Maybe you are furrowing your brow right now, thinking, *"I believe, but I don't feel like God is inside me."* Relax. If you believe, He is there. The more you read the Bible, pray and share with other Christians, the more you'll see the Holy Spirit at work in your life. He guides you where to go, corrects you when you mess up and gives you a glimmer of things to come. When you have peace in the midst of chaos, strength at the heart of your weakness and guidance when you can't see where you're going, that's the Holy Spirit at work.

Perhaps in your grief you have come to understand God within you as never before. You see, the Holy Spirit within you yearns for that victory party, renews your faith and helps you to breathe again.

Picture Jesus in His heavenly throne room, sitting

and desperately…

at the right hand of God. But Jesus is sitting on the very edge of His seat. He's fidgeting in His chair, smiling down on all of us: His long-awaited guests. Then He grabs His Dad's arm and points toward the door. He asks, "May I go now, Dad? May I go get them now?"

God smiles and says, "Not yet, Son, just a little bit longer."

Jesus sits back in His chair for a little while. Then He sweetly asks God again, "How about now?"

Maybe the throne room of the Lord God Almighty is a little more regal than this, but I have no doubt that Jesus is just itching to come down here and take us home the split second His Dad says, "OK, Son, it's time."

...listening for the

doorbell to ring."

Now the **dwelling** of **God** is with **men,** and *He* will *live* with *them.*

They will be His people, and *God Himself* will be **with them** and be their **God.**

He will wipe
every tear
from their eyes.

There will be
no more
death
or **mourning**
or **crying**
or **pain,**

for the
old order of things
has
passed away.

Revelation 21:3–4

A Meeting With Jesus: Brian's Story

I will never forget lying in that empty bed, thinking, *"What just happened to me? How could life be so perfect 12 hours ago and now everything has changed?"* There I was, only 25 years old, remembering the police officer's face when he said my wife Tatia had died in a car accident.

Tatia dying was like someone had drawn a jagged line through my body and suddenly knocked half of it off. With that half of me missing, I didn't know what to do. I had been a type "A" personality, but when that officer spoke, all of my goals and dreams immediately vanished, because I could accomplish none of them without her.

I met Tatia in 1993, my sophomore year of college, at a music and theater department get-together. I was hesitant to go because I was a sports guy and not really into the arts. I'm glad I went, though, because that evening everything changed. Meeting Tatia was the first time in my life that I felt like I wasn't pretending to be someone I was not. Her genuineness made me completely honest and open—like she was already a great friend. And so we talked the whole night; I just knew that this girl was different.

Dating Tatia meant everything from ice-skating and walks in the park to college football and basketball games. We did normal, everyday things. It was the quality of the time we spent together that counted. We enjoyed being around each other so much it didn't matter what we did.

I graduated in the spring of 1995 and Tatia graduated in December. A week or two before Christmas, I decided it was "that time," so I went shopping and bought a really nice, brown leather briefcase for her new job—and an engagement ring. When she opened up the briefcase, she dug through it and found the ring. Her jaw dropped; she was not expecting it at all. We were giggly, knowing that no matter what happened from that point forward, we could do it together.

After we got married in the fall of 1996, Tatia became a development officer at a university, and I became a financial planner, selling life insurance and other financial products. Married life was great. We became so meshed and so unified in our everyday life that our thoughts and goals were completely on the same page. Since our careers were going great, we bought some land to build a house. Tatia worked with the architect to design it the way she wanted. We talked about starting a family and could hardly wait to bring a child into our new home.

I can't describe how perfect our lives were. I remember sharing with some friends at work, "We are so blessed. We have great wives; we have great families; we have great careers, making great money. We're in a Christian business, working for a Fortune 500 company. How much better could life be?" I'll never forget that conversation.

On Tuesday, July 7, 1998, I came home for dinner. I had an appointment at 6:30 p.m. and Tatia had a senior high youth group meeting at our church. When I left that night, I gave her a hug and a kiss and said, "I love you and I'll see you later." Saying goodbye couldn't have been more perfect.

Tatia was on her way to her meeting, on a two-lane road, when a massive thunderstorm hit. The heavy rain prevented her from seeing a car brake unexpectedly in front of her, and when Tatia hit her brakes, her car hydroplaned into the opposite lane, where she was T-boned by an SUV going 60 miles per hour. She died instantly. No one else was hurt.

It was after 10:00 p.m. by the time the police officer had taken me to the crash site and then the funeral home to see her. They had her in a back room, on a table covered with a sheet up to her neck. I remember crying as I kissed her forehead and fell on my knees praying. I wondered how I was ever going to live without her.

The reality of the whole thing started to sink in. The person who had affected my life the most and made me a better person was gone. I knew of only one place to turn: *"Jesus,"* I prayed, *"I need Your help. You will have to carry me because I can't do this alone."*

Jesus picked me up and threw me over His shoulders, like a sack of potatoes, and said, "Come on. Let's go. I will carry you for as long as you need to be carried."

After Tatia's memorial service, I lived one day at a time. I couldn't look ahead beyond that. I felt so alone, like I was the only one going through this, especially when my friends started to resume their normal lives again. I felt as though I was in this fog and on the other side was God's plan for me, shining like a white light. I also remember thinking, *"I really want to know what God has planned, but if I know, I'm probably going to freak out and not want to do it. I guess I'll just have to be patient."* At the time, I was not very good at being patient.

When Tatia died, we were two weeks away from breaking ground, so I went ahead and built the house. The work helped to keep my mind occupied, but once it was done, our list of things to do together was also done. The house was our last dream together.

My family and co-workers started to question me about when I was going to get back to work again, but I just couldn't do it. After all, I was in the life insurance business, and Tatia was my first death claim. My mom would ask, "Where's that fire? Where's that spark of energy that made you successful in all the things you've wanted to accomplish in life?"

My answer was, "You can't start a fire when the wood is wet." That's the way I was living life back then. My life was soaking wet, and there was no way I was going to start a fire with wet wood!

After I took a couple of months off, I started doing some joint sales work with a couple of my friends to try and get back into the rhythm again. But that meant every night I was having a two- to four-hour discussion about Tatia's accident with clients, and why they should protect their families. It's like I was right there again. If people said, "No," I wanted to reach across and say, *"Don't you get it? Don't you understand what can happen to you in a split second?"*

But I was trying to make the job work. My company's state conference happened to fall on the anniversary of when Tatia and I started dating. I was having a rough day, bawling and crying. In the middle of the night, I looked over into the corner of the room and saw an image of Tatia's face. Just her face. It was not a ghost. It was like an energy field. I wasn't looking for it, nor had I ever seen anything like it. I felt no anxiety or fear; I remember feeling this overwhelming peace. It was the comfort that could have only come from God. It felt as though He was saying, "You can do this. I'm right here beside you. Keep going." I was amazed, but since then, many grieving people have shared with me similar experiences.

When I woke up the next morning, I knew I had seen a glimmer of light through the fog. God expected me to keep going without knowing where, except to follow Him. I had always had faith in Christ, but rarely had I lived my life waiting for God to show me the way. I had never understood waiting on God to let me know the right decision in my life. All of this stuff about God communicating with me, or working through my heart, was completely new. I had always set goals, made plans and charged off to succeed in them. Now I had no clue where I was headed; I had to wait on God to lead me.

Later that morning at the conference, I had the opportunity to share about the accident and reassure everyone that I was going to be OK. There wasn't a dry eye in the room, including my own. Afterward, my company asked me to speak at other conferences. Each time, people came flooding up to share their own personal story with me. They talked about losing a parent, caring for a sick child or knowing a friend with cancer. I saw all this brokenness, and knew each person felt so alone. Talking about my story gave others the courage to express their emotions. In telling my story, I began to see that as much as I missed Tatia, I had become a completely different person because of the impact she had made on my life. I was now able to help others find the comfort that I had received from God.

I knew that Tatia had wanted to be cremated rather than have a burial, so I needed to decide what to do with her ashes. Since she had lived in Germany for most of her childhood, and that is where she called home, I decided to spread her ashes over the Rhine River on our wedding anniversary. I had crawled into a hole mentally that day, and before I took her box of ashes to the river and let her go through my fingertips, I lay in the hotel room, crying and talking out loud to God. Yes, I had grieved, and, yes, I had prayed, but at that particular moment I threw myself at the feet of Jesus and said to Him, *"All right, what's going on here? What's my sorry butt still doing here on earth? How do I move forward now, when everything has been wiped away? Why couldn't I have done what You needed me to do the other way? When Tatia and I were married, I felt so strong, like I could conquer the*

21

world. Why can't I live for You from a position of strength instead of a place of vulnerability?"

As I cried out to Jesus in that hotel room, I didn't understand that I wasn't ready to do what God had planned for me. My faith needed to be stronger to pull that plan off. It was like Tatia was an angel here on earth.

God had sent her to get me to a certain point, and then I had to go on my own. Over time, God led me to understand that He was always with me, every day of my life, not just when my wife died in a car accident. Through my grief, God was laying a new foundation for me on top of the old foundation that Christ had given me since childhood.

About a year after the accident, I decided to transfer to Nashville and start over. I was miserable living in that huge dream house by myself. I couldn't stay focused on my work; everywhere I went I saw constant reminders of "Brian and Tatia." I needed a change of scenery and to be close to friends who understood what I was going through.

My friend Jennie had moved to Nashville to pursue music. Our paths had crossed earlier, at just the right time — God's time. Tatia and I knew Jennie from college. She dated a friend of mine and sang in the school choir with Tatia. After Tatia's death, the empathy that I felt from Jennie was amazing. She had experienced several deaths in her life, and told me, "If you ever want to talk to somebody, I'll help you out anyway that I can." That's how our friendship really got started. When I moved to Nashville, it was purely as a friend, but over time, we saw in each other who we both wanted to be.

Starting a new relationship was far from easy. I prayed to God, *"Here's this girl I love and who loves me, and yet I have all this baggage. How do we ever make this work?"* Every time Jennie drove in a thunderstorm or was late coming home, my anxiety kicked in. I was afraid. If I could lose someone I loved once, there's no reason it couldn't happen again. It took time and lots of talking, but we finally got through the baggage and were able to start dealing with the fun stuff in life.

The fog lifted on the day Jennie and I were married. Marrying Jennie gave me all the courage and strength I needed to move forward and build a stronger life and a stronger faith. I had a purpose and a responsibility beyond myself now. Four years later, we were blessed with Emma Lou, our daughter.

God used Jennie's music to radically change my life. After being invited to sing in church, Jennie was hired to record Scripture-based music for a project. She wrote a song "*Let not Your Heart be Troubled.*" This song spoke so powerfully to the brokenhearted that I knew it could touch many lives. We had just built a new home and bought two new cars, but I quit my job and became part owner of a company to promote Jennie's CD and other Scripture-based music. I spoke to my old life insurance company, and they bought the CD to go into the condolences kit for all their beneficiaries. The rest is history.

The music and my newest company — AriSon Records — are both very successful. We've sold over 500,000 CDs throughout the U.S. and to countries all over the world. Today I have a team of over 20 people that works with me in making this music come alive — from songwriting to vocal recording, to touring to office support. By promoting this music at various conferences, concert venues and churches, I have shared my story with tens of thousands of people.

God has finally given me a chance to use all the things He had prepared me for after Tatia's death. Everything I have done has been a response to God's will, not my own decisions. I have waited every step of the way to understand God's plan for me. And He has been there, trustworthy and true. Through God alone, our music has taken His Word to 1.5 million lives. Praise God!

There is no way to prepare for the death of a loved one, whether you have a chance to say good-bye or not. You can't live in fear of what's going to happen tomorrow. I can't live in fear over whether I'm going to have Jennie for another day or another 80 years. All I can do is live today to the fullest with her and pray that tomorrow she is going to be here with me.

Life can change at any moment. When Tatia was gone, I missed the little things so much. Now I take time to smell Jennie's hair, touch the warmth of her skin or feel the embrace of our daughter's arms around my neck. I believe that God is in everything that happens to me. He always has been; He always will be.

Jesus,

Your **VICTORY** *over*
sin & death

means everything.

YOU

are my *HOPE*
and my *STRENGTH.*

Wash me *clean*
of my doubts
& let me *taste*
the splendor of
Your glory
now *and* forevermore.

Amen

Can you hardly wait?

Chapter Two

Why Can't I Get On With My Life?

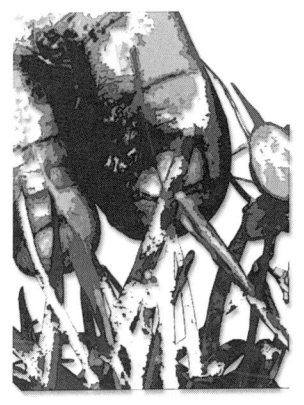

*An unexpected
and undeserved*
**new
beginning**

Bare Feet
Always Get Dirty

The funeral is over and everyone has gone home. You are more than just lost; you are physically, mentally and emotionally exhausted. The ordeal of making arrangements was enough to wear down the strongest of souls, but long before the funeral, exhaustion became your way of life. The weeks, months or even years before a loved one's death often include a season of sacrifice: your sacrifice.

You may not recall how this season of sacrifice began. Someone had to organize the meds, schedule doctor appointments and think of ways to make your loved one smile. You didn't volunteer to make the medical or financial decisions; you just did it. Whether your involvement arose from a physical illness, mental illness, addiction or just because someone needed you, giving is exhausting.

Of course, it's not like your other demands disappeared. An assortment of laundry, pets, groceries, meals, work and family members waited for your attention as well. Being you, you placed the needs of others before your own for so long you didn't even notice you had forgotten your needs. Self-sacrifice felt normal — like a way of life instead of a season of life. You barely noticed it anymore. That's kind of the way it was with dirty feet and me.

Growing up in North Florida, I developed the attitude that shoes were optional and dirty feet were a way of life. In the summer, I looked for tadpoles *barefoot*, played kickball *barefoot* and even built forts in the woods *barefoot*. By the end of the day it was hard to tell where my feet stopped and the ground began. My mom often shouted, "Hose off those feet before you come inside this house, young lady!"

I was always too busy playing to notice something as mundane as mud squished between my toes. And, if I had noticed, I wouldn't have stopped to get cleaned up. Well, just think. Would you leave a kick-ball game (especially if you're winning) or abandon your handmade fort to wash a pair of dirty feet? I didn't think so! So I just kept playing, mud and all.

You'll agree that none of us go outside *just* to get our feet dirty. Dirty feet happen as we try to drudge through life the best way we know how. Dirt is the result of the world happening to us. Our exhaustion, self-doubt, worry, frustration and anger leave a smudge of dirt, or worse, a splotch of mud. After a while, it piles up on us. Unfortunately, most of us are too busy to notice when we need a good foot washing.

Even though Jesus didn't have the benefit of my garden hose, He was a foot washer (John 13). Actually, He is still washing feet today. Yet somehow foot washing hardly seems appropriate for the King of Kings and Lord of Lords. So why does He do it? Why does He kneel down before us with towel and basin and remove our banged up shoes and well-worn socks? Why does Jesus hold our feet in His gentle hands and wash every callous, blister and damaged toenail? Because He knows what walking through a season of sacrifice can do to a pair of feet.

You may not realize how difficult your season of sacrifice has been for you, but Jesus sees each time you stub your toe, scrape your foot or stumble to the ground, too tired to move. That's why He's not willing to leave you there, hurting and weary. Part of you may want to stay there. But let's face it: Getting on with your life means letting Jesus give you a new beginning.

When your loved one died, you felt barely alive yourself. You had no thoughts about your future. You simply survived. Then, at some point in your grieving, you felt a subtle sense of relief. This relief reached beyond knowing that your loved one was safely at home in heaven with Christ. This relief came because the burden of your season of sacrifice had been lifted. Before, you had poured out your time and energy on your loved one. Now where was all of that unspent energy to go?

Realizing that you actually have choices, you consider returning to activities you gave up during your season of sacrifice, or maybe some new outings, new friendships or even an adventure or two. The relieved part of you feels tantalized about the possibilities. Maybe, just maybe, you can make a new beginning. Whether you realize it or not, this hope is the first drop of water from the basin Jesus empties over your path-worn feet. Feeling startled but refreshed, you begin to notice how beat up your feet are; your hope for a future pours a sweet relief on your aching feet.

Then, suddenly, the shadow of a future without your loved one falls across your heart. Thoughts of Jesus and tomorrow disappear; you're overcome by guilt — raging, all-encompassing guilt. From deep

"From Christ's

inside you cry out, *"I don't want to do new things or regain old things! I just want my loved one back! I want my loved one back, right here, today!"* You willingly reject the promise of hope so you can grasp your grief tightly to your chest. Why, you'd gladly face another season of sacrifice just to see your loved one again.

But Jesus says, "It's time for a new season. It's time for a season of comfort—not of giving comfort—but of receiving comfort."

On the surface, comfort does sounds appealing, but you have no thought that you need comfort yourself. Your focus is on being strong. Friends may try to comfort you, but every touch on the shoulder or sincere expression of concern finds you stiffening up and acting strong. You may be thinking, *"If I don't, what will happen?"* I guess that's the question. What might happen if you do let yourself be comforted? If you fall apart one more time, will you get back up? Or will the desire to stay in your bed rolled in a ball finally win? Deciding to get on with your life boils down to this: Does the sorrow of your grief feel safer

comfort comes…

than the fear of a new beginning?

Jesus won't leave you in your grief, no matter how much you want to stay there. *From Christ's comfort comes God's peace, which — through no act of your own — gives birth to hope.* Look at that last sentence. You throw yourself at Jesus in prayer. Then, when you've emptied yourself out at His feet, you find peace. You know this peace comes from God, because it makes no sense. Everything in this world says you should feel miserable, but instead you feel peace. And this peace is so filled with Christ, my friend, that you sense the faint, sweet brush of hope.

You see, whether welcomed or unwelcomed, God rains down new beginnings on us all the time. That's the true meaning of the cross: Christ died so He can wash us clean, breathe in us a new life and send us out to discover the joy of walking with Him. It's undeserved and unearned. You may be thinking, *"I've already done that with God. He's already saved me."* God wants more for you than an eternal life with Him. He wants you to live *now* and to live abundantly!

…God's peace, which

This might scare you, but God's new beginnings are not a one-time deal. God rains down new beginnings on you fresh every morning, every moment. God is a God of faithfulness. He has sent His Son to wash you clean and give you hope. Christ will stop at nothing — not your grief, not your depression and not your loneliness — to breathe new life into you. That's how much He loves you. That's how much Jesus feels your pain and yearns for your joy.

So why does Jesus wash feet? So He can show you the full extent of His love (John 13:1). Imagine the full extent of Jesus' love raining down on you. Don't let the condition of your feet embarrass you. Place them in Jesus' loving hands so He can heal and restore them. Let Him carry you through a season of comfort into an unexpected and undeserved new beginning.

gives birth to hope."

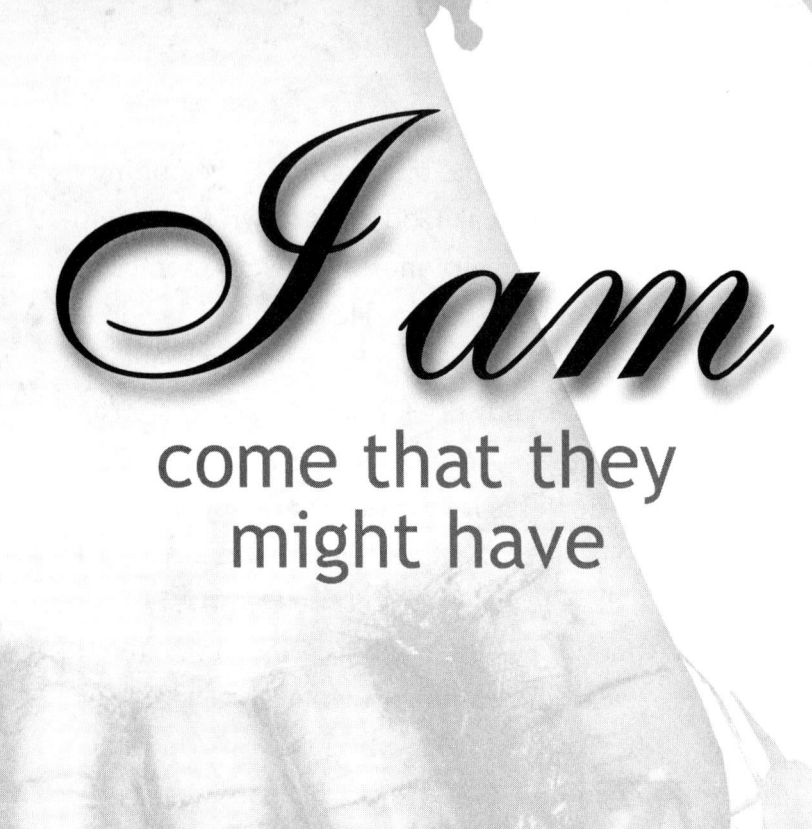

I am

come that they
might have

life,
and
that they
might have it more
abundantly.

John 10:10

A Meeting With Jesus:
Kate's Story

When the doctor said, "Kate, there's something wrong with your heart," I felt that it had broken open and lay empty. The diagnosis was small artery disease, but the cause ran much deeper. For the last 10 years I had dealt with death, but I had not stopped once to grieve for myself. First, Dad died, then my father-in-law and now Mom. I had focused on taking care of everyone else: my parents, my children and my husband. And I'm glad I did. Yet now my heart was literally broken from overwork and grief.

My dad put it this way, "Kate, you give and give and then you pray for strength to give more." That's what I'd done. But what do I do next? "Next" had always meant taking care of someone else. Now I needed to take care of me.

Taking care of things as I grew up with two sisters was a way for me to feel needed. I was 10 when my sister, Gail, was born; I was taking care of her by myself at 12. I'd meet Mom at the bus stop every afternoon, where she passed Gail off to me as she got on the bus to work the second shift. I watched Gail until Dad got home, and then I finished the supper Mom had started. My sister, Terry, was four years older. For some reason, it never dawned on me that she should be in charge instead of me.

My life didn't change much when I married my first husband at 19 and had two great boys. The marriage ended when my youngest was nine.

After another nine years as a single mom, I met Johnnie. Johnnie made me laugh, and as a struggling single mom, laughter had been a rare commodity. He valued me and completely won me over with his winning smile and generosity.

I knew Johnnie and I were partners for life, even though he had rheumatoid arthritis. I was a physical therapist, so I knew what I was getting into. I understood this lifelong decision included helping him through his physical struggles. Johnnie's illness has led us to endure his two knee replacements, two hip replacements, a shoulder replacement and reconstruction on the tendons in his hand. But my husband's determination and optimism in the face of any pain or procedure has, thankfully, never failed him.

I've taken care of others my whole life, but the last 10 years have been the most difficult. In 1998, my mom began to develop Alzheimer's. My dad was ill too, struggling with Chronic Obstructive Pulmonary Disease. I was the one who forced Dad to recognize Mom's failing health.

One day at a restaurant, Mom became disoriented after using the bathroom; she couldn't find her way back to the table. I said, "Daddy, turn around and watch her with the eyes of someone that doesn't know her." I had to make him acknowledge how lost she'd become.

Dad said, "OK, we'll go to the doctor, but you have to go with us."

After Mom was diagnosed and placed on meds, Dad's health took a turn for the worse. I received three calls in the middle of the night because he couldn't breathe. Mom's deterioration from Alzheimer's made it impossible for Dad to depend on her help in an emergency. It was then Johnnie and I hired a contractor to build an apartment for them in our basement. Dad died of congestive heart failure two weeks before it was completed, so we moved Mom in with us ASAP.

The light went out for Mom when Dad died. Having Mom live with me was like adopting a child. She was completely disoriented after leaving the house she'd lived in for 37 years. She needed help with everything from putting on her pajamas to brushing her teeth. On a good day she knew the toothbrush was for brushing her teeth.

Mom's health continued to worsen. A caregiver took over while I was at work, but I was "it" when I got home. My sleep was shallow and interrupted by Mom getting lost during nighttime trips to the bathroom. I was dead tired, but I had to keep going.

In all of this, God was so there, so present. When I began what I call "screaming crying" — not just crying, but screaming crying — and I'd finally fall down exhausted, His still small voice would speak to me. One time, as I lay crying, He said, "You didn't read your devotional today." I opened it up and read, *"Do not lean on your own understanding."* Period. God knew I needed that verse on that day. This verse became my mantra.

Something had to change. So in early 2002, I put Mom in a nursing home. I couldn't take care of her anymore — not physically, emotionally or financially. We had gone through most of her and Dad's money to pay the daytime caregivers.

Every time I went to visit her, Mom begged to come home. I tried to explain that I just couldn't care for her now and that these people were experts at what she needed. But she cried, "You just don't love me!"

God gave me a priceless gift one day. After hearing Mom's pleas to take her home, I fell on the floor and screamed, "God! Why is this happening? You can get through to her mind. You have to convince her that I do love her. I love her beyond measure. I just can't do this anymore."

Then, when I was totally exhausted, I heard a voice in my head say, "Now she sees dimly, but when she is with Me, I'm going to tell her everything." I looked around and knew I had heard God. I claimed this promise many times in years to come.

My load didn't lift, even with Mom in a nursing home. In the fall of 2002, my father-in law, Joe, had a heart attack and congestive heart failure. So Joe and his wife, Lucille, moved off their farm and stayed with us for a few months.

A short time later, Joe went back into the hospital. But once in hospice care, his heart began to fail. By the time everyone else had said their goodbyes, it was just Johnnie, Lucille and me. We nursed and loved him to the other side. Not even leaving to get the nurse when he passed, we just sat with him, finishing our goodbyes.

We urged Lucille to stay with us for a while, but when summer came, she went back to the farm. In the fall, her neighbor called. He was worried about Lucille, so he broke into the house and found her on the floor. She had suffered a stroke.

The stroke took the sight in her right eye and affected her balance. After rehab, she moved in with us. The little apartment in the basement has worked out well for her. She still cooks in the little kitchen downstairs and usually has dinner with us.

In May of 2007, my mother began to decline rapidly. You don't die of Alzheimer's; you die of everything that Alzheimer's shuts down. She was beginning to refuse food and liquids. As she became agitated, I told the staff, "The Tylenol is not working anymore." So they started morphine drops. She died peacefully the next day, surrounded by her family.

One of Mom's last words before she died was "Home". After six years in nursing homes, Mom never stopped asking to go home. That's a hard one to live with. But even though Mom never stopped saying I didn't love her, I knew that God understood and that He would tell her. And when she died, I thought at last, she's home.

My relief was short-lived. After Mom died, I shut down. It's odd. I had grieved so much about Mom for 10 years that I thought things would be easier. I expected to feel a lot better than I did. There was relief that she was with Daddy and that she finally understood why I couldn't bring her home. But I also felt such insurmountable exhaustion that I could barely function. I was spent.

A week or so after Mom's funeral, I lay down in that exhausted state and began to talk with God. As I asked Him how to get past this heavy feeling of exhaustion, I fell asleep. That is when I had a dream that is still clear as a bell. In it, Jesus stood nearby as I walked into a beautiful, green valley. I heard Jesus say, "Kate, the 23rd Psalm is not just for the dying. I want you to understand that I have brought you — **you** — through the valley of the shadow of death." Then I noticed we were next to a stream. "And now it's time for you to lie down beside still waters so I can restore your soul." As I lay down, I felt peaceful for the first time in years. I finally understood that I couldn't make the fatigue go away by myself. God was going to have to heal me. I woke up crying.

The dream was empowering for me because I could finally let go. It was not empowering because God had made me strong, but because I received permission to be weak. I could lie down and rest because God was going to heal me, heal my soul.

For the first time in my life, I'm really grieving. I'm not just grieving the loss of my mom; I'm grieving the loss of my dad that I buried deep inside 10 years ago so I could care for others. Through the grief, I've found myself in this precious time. It's a time of going inward and finding Christ in my life — not my life connected to someone else's, but finding how Christ is connected to my life and my life alone. It's time for me to figure out how to be a caregiver and take care of myself at the same time. Maybe God wants me to care for others, but in a way that is less self-depleting. As I prayed recently, God said, *"How does the word "nurturer" sound to you, Kate?"* Better. I like the sound of that much better than being a caregiver.

In the process, I have begun to set fragile boundaries. I say, "No," when I mean no and stick with it. I've prayed for grace to set those boundaries in a loving way.

At first people said, "What's wrong with you? You've really changed."

I answer, "Yes, I have." No one can go through what I've been through and not be changed.

I get comments like, "You're so moody," and "For heaven sakes, Kate, it's been nine months." Someone even said that my mom would be very upset with me over all this "moping around." I guess I always appeared to have things so together. Didn't anyone notice I was drowning?

Now I let my weaknesses show. This must be scary for some people in my life. My feelings about these relationships haven't changed, but the way I relate to others definitely needed to change. I feel freer now to relate to others from a whole new perspective — not just from how I can be of help to them, but by exploring the other great aspects of being in relationships.

Sometimes I wonder if taking care of myself is being Christ-like, because it feels so self-absorbed. But if I don't learn to nurture myself now, I will miss the lessons of the last 10 years. And I have a genuine, deep sense about my grief and my heart condition. If I miss this, I could go to an early grave. Is that what Christ has in mind for me? Only He knows, but the doctors say my heart will be fine, if I take better care of it. I'm going with that.

I wouldn't trade the last 10 months since Mom's death for anything. Since I've taken time to reflect on my life and my relationship with Christ, the rewards have been incredible. I continue to be blessed with insights, dreams, books and songs that have taken on new meanings.

The one boundary I've completely let down is the one between God and me. He is in control of my life. I've told Him, *"You are the only way I am going to get through this,"* and, in response, I have been rewarded over and over by His presence in my walk through this valley.

Blessed Christ,

I place my *grief* into
Your waiting *hands.*

Wash me **clean,**
fill me with Your **peace** and
breathe in me a new **hope.**

Take the **blessings**
I received from
my loved one
and **use them** to form...

a
NEW BEGINNING
for me
...in You.

Amen

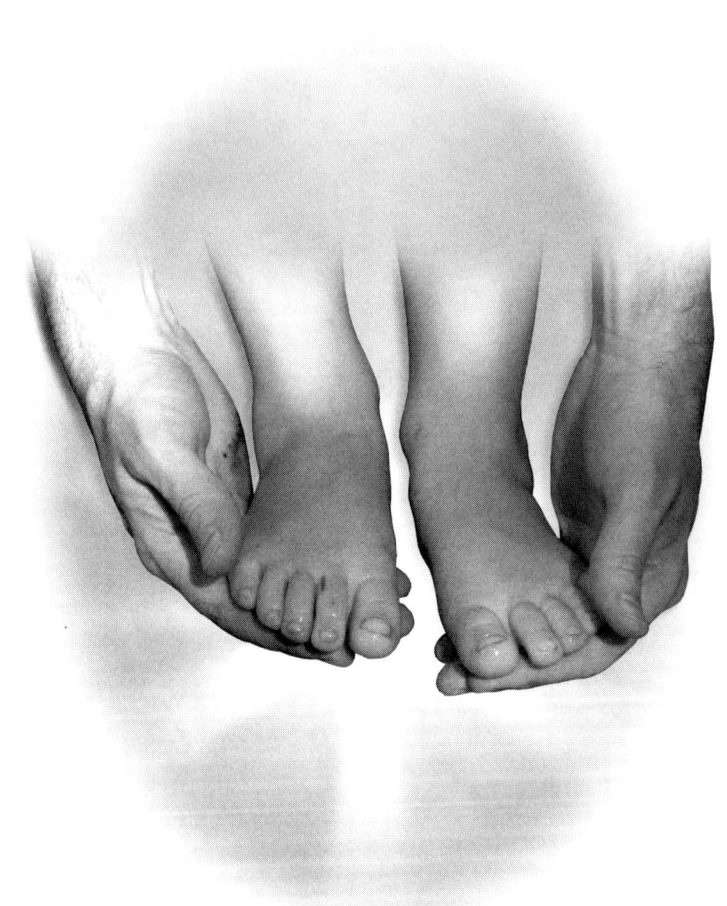

Let Him give you a new beginning!

Chapter Three

Why Did You Let Them Die?

Truly **trusting** *God*
comes from
knowing
who He is

How Waves
Work

$\mathscr{E}$ach of us, in our own way, has known love. But sometimes your life is struck with a love that envelops your very spirit. Knowing that you have been blessed with such a love can leave you humbled. You may realize you have such a love when you hold your firstborn in your arms, when the look of a friend becomes the gaze of a beloved or as you stand at the altar saying your vows. This type of love fills your every breath. You have given yourself to this love with no restraints, no holding back. Yet to give completely to such a love always leaves a touch of fear. *"What if something happens to my loved one?"*

How can you not fear, when the thought of living without this child, without this spouse or without this friend or parent is your worst nightmare? Even when everyone appears healthy and safe, that fear can creep in. You turn to God and beg, *"Please take me, Lord. My loved one's life is worth 10 of mine. Leave him on this earth to bless others as he has blessed me."*

You tell God logically, emotionally and emphatically that your life would decay without your loved one. You know God heard you. Life goes on and you rest assured, knowing that God is gracious and merciful. Surely God won't take my loved one from me.

Then your worst nightmare comes true. Someone you love on this earth more than your own breath has died, and you are left dumbstruck. You don't know how to breathe. How can you not ask God, *"Why? I prayed, I begged and yet You left me here alone."* Since this death, nothing seems right. Things you thought you understood about God, you now question. You ask God, *"Why did You let my loved one die?"* Your search for understanding deteriorates into blaming yourself: *"God must be doing this because of me."* That's not true.

Please don't let yourself be swallowed by senseless self-blame. Your loved one's death was not meant to teach you a lesson, to punish you for your past or to make you a better person. God doesn't work that way. He doesn't bring sin or death to a life. Sin and death come from living in this tainted world. But *every* life and *every* death is used by God to complete His perfect plan: to bring His precious children to live with Him for all eternity.

Don't get me wrong, salvation is a good plan, but why can't God's plan save this lost world *and* provide a just world? Each of us can look at the world and see the injustice God needs to fix. How hard can it be for the God of the universe to stop the senseless deaths? All you're asking for is justice now, not in heaven.

Can't God see that a vibrant, young mother of two needs to live and a person hopelessly in a coma, incapacitated and suffering needs to go home to Jesus? That seems fair. I bet not a day goes by when a person with a long, full life begs God to die so an innocent child can live. Why not answer that prayer?

Of course, through our eyes justice can look very black and white until the questions get tougher. Is it just for a man who donates a lot of money to live or one that donates a lot of time? What about the six-year-old who lives down your street or the one on the opposite side of the world? See what I mean about tough questions? Do you really want your life and the lives of those you love lengthened or shortened by our feeble human understanding of justice?

The truth is, none of us deserve life because each of us has done things wrong, every last human on the planet. That's why Jesus took the punishment for everything we've done wrong. Now we are not judged based on what we deserve but on what we have been given: God's grace and boundless mercy.

This is God's plan.

No question, God's plan can be hard to see. The truth is, you can't step far enough back to see any situation with the clarity of God. From everything you can see, the death of your loved one is wrong. He should still be right here, by your side. No matter how hard you try, you can't find the clarity to see God's purpose. You look at the world and see chaos. God looks at the world and sees His purpose woven through all things. God never brings sin and death to a life, but He will take all the wrongs and ultimately make them right. Let's face it. It comes down to trust. Do you trust that God knows what He's doing?

Of course, there are many kinds of trust. You trust your car to start tomorrow morning. When driving down a two-lane road at 50 mph, you trust the car coming toward you to stay in its lane. You trust the teachers at school to return your child to you safe and sound. This trust builds each time you have driven past another car or picked up your child from

"She learned to

school, and everything was fine. You learned to trust. Of course, all you have to do is watch the news to know you can trust others only up to a point.

Hebrews 2:13 talks of trusting God with an *inward certainty.* Think about that. You can't trust another person with an inward certainty, even those you love, because they're fallible. God is infallible. Yet truly trusting God comes from knowing who He is, regardless of the things that are happening around you. So who is He? God is love without end. He adores you! He relishes your victories and cries in your pain. He is all-powerful, all-faithful and all-forgiving. God never breaks a promise, because it is His nature, His very essence, to be *completely* trustworthy. God is who He says He is, and He will do what He says He will do.

The problem comes when you want God to be different. This is often true when you're grieving. Maybe you want God to put your purpose before His, or you want Him to reveal His goodness in all situations. You could just want Him to impact the

trust the waves...

world in a way that makes sense to you. *"If the pain and the death in my life do not make sense, then I need God to be different."*

Are you asking God to stop being God? Are you asking God to put your needs before His purpose? Or can you trust God to be who He says He is, no matter what? Trusting things to be unchanging can be a tough lesson. My friend Linda learned this lesson at her first trip to the beach.

I grew up in Florida, about 25 minutes from the beach. When I was 15, Linda moved to town from Pittsburgh. I was stunned to discover that she had never been in the ocean, so I immediately made plans to correct this heinous oversight. She knew how to swim, but swimming in a pool or a lake is not the same as swimming in the ocean.

At the beach that next weekend, after applying large quantities of sunscreen to her extremely white skin, we joyfully ran into the ocean. The waves were big and rolling — just right for body surfing. Just as we passed knee deep, a large wave approached us.

...*to do exactly*

As I proceeded to jump over the wave, I turned to see Linda, standing stiff as a tree and taking the wave full in her face. She came up sputtering and gasping, but before I could tell her to jump over the waves, another was upon her. Just when she was able to take a breath, she found herself back under the water, wondering what had just hit her. I pulled her up off her bottom, and after she realized she was all right and had a good laugh, Linda learned her first lesson on how to swim in the ocean. Since I had grown up around waves, I never dreamed I'd have to explain to anyone that you either jump over the wave or dive under the wave unless you want to get plowed down by the wave.

By the end of our fun-filled day at the beach, Linda knew with an inward certainty that no amount of hoping or wishing was going to stop the waves from coming. She learned to trust the waves to do exactly what waves do: they just keep on coming.

You see, God just keeps on being God whether or not we understand what He is doing. The Bible says

what waves do:

we are to trust in the Lord with all our heart and to not lean on our own understanding (Proverbs 3:5). Now, I don't know about you, but I like leaning on my own understanding! I want to see with my eyes and touch with my hands, and most of all, I want to understand with my mind, the things I trust. I want to understand God. If we could understand what God is doing, we could trust Him so much easier! But, let's face it, if we did understand God, we would not be trusting Him with an inward certainty.

Inward certainty is not something that comes easily, especially if you are feeling distant from God right now. You may not know God's purpose in the loss of your loved one, but maybe you can start to trust God based on what you *do* know. Have you felt peace in the midst of chaos? That's God. Have you seen beauty and joy beyond compare? That's God. Have you felt strength when you were swallowed with weakness? That's God, too. He is right there in your life, reaching out to hold you close. Trust in what you know about God; don't hold back. Feel His

they just

arms supporting you, His precious voice soothing you and His tears melting into your own. Let go of the space between you and God. Just like the waves, He is coming for you, now and always.

keep on coming."

Trust in the **_LORD_** with all your **_heart_** and **_lean not_** on your own **_understanding;_**

in **ALL** your ways
acknowledge
Him,

and **He** will make your

PATHS

STRAIGHT.

Proverbs 3:5–6

A Meeting With Jesus: Sharon's Story

As a mother, you try to prepare your kids for the challenges they will face in life. But you never think you'll need to prepare them to die. On the first day of school or a trip to the dentist, you tell them what to expect. What do you say to your five-year-old son about how to die? In December 1975, when I was 27 years old, my son Jeff was diagnosed with Burkitt's lymphoma. At that time, no one with Burkitt's lymphoma had ever lived to adulthood.

My husband Mike and I had just moved into a new house with our three kids: Steve, 6; Jeff, 5; and Marla, 1. Jeff's weight loss, sluggishness and bowel problems were the first signs that something was wrong. I made the doctor appointment, hoping it was just school stress, but part of me knew something was seriously wrong. Still, when the pediatrician said, "There's a mass in his abdomen, and I need you to take him to the hospital right now," I was so frightened I could barely think.

People say, "I don't think I could stand to find

out that one of my kids had cancer." I was no different.

When they told me Jeff had Burkitt's lymphoma, I was on the top floor of the hospital, looking out a window. I was so desperate, I thought, *"If I could just jump out, this would all be over."* But I couldn't. Yet how in the world could I go back in that hospital room with a happy face and reassure my little boy that everything's going to be OK?

"We are quite sure that this is cancer," the doctor said, "but we're going to make an incision in his stomach and take a look at it." After 20 minutes in the operating room, the doctor came out and told us, "It's everywhere, in the abdomen, in the intestines. There's nothing we can do except try some treatments."

Since there were very few patients with Burkitt's lymphoma at that time, they treated Jeff like a leukemia patient. That meant watching my kindergartener cope with nausea from the chemotherapy, exhaustion from the radiation and bad dreams from the meds. Besides those side effects, the bone marrow extraction and the spinal taps caused excruciating pain. Jeff hated them. We'd get in the car to go to the hospital and he'd say, "I don't think they're going to give me one today."

And I'd say, "I don't think they will either." I tried so hard to keep him from worrying. After the procedures began, he would cry and I would cry. They'd put Jeff in a fetal position and have me hold him close while they injected him. The pain was unbearable.

When the procedure was done, Jeff would say, "Do you think we could look at the toys after this?"

I'd say, "Of course! You can get anything you want. Anything!" At the store, Jeff would pick out some little toy that didn't amount to anything, but it seemed to help him forget about the pain and just go on.

I learned a lot from Jeff. He was so loving and kind, and he never complained about his illness or treatments. One time Jeff's big brother Steve found him hiding in the closet. Jeff just said, "I don't want Mom to know I'm hurting." It just broke me to realize everything my little boy was going through, and he was worried about me.

To be honest, between the negative prognosis, the painful procedures and watching Jeff's little body struggle to stay alive, I thought I was going to crumble. Looking at Jeff lying in the hospital bed with no hair and all the monitors on, I felt so alone, so abandoned. Mike's parents would come and console him, but my parents couldn't comfort me. I remember even telling my mom and dad, "I think it's getting bad, and you need to come."

Mom and Dad told me, "We can't. You're stronger than we are; you take care of it."

It was like I couldn't find anybody — *anybody* — who was going to speak something good into my life. There was no one to say, "You're going to be OK," or "God's going to take care of you," or something else I could hold onto. I was falling apart; I was completely helpless.

But somebody had to be strong for Jeff, so I called out to God, *"My husband can't fix it, my parents can't fix it; You have to help me here. This little boy is counting on me, and I am totally dependent on You."* I felt God pick me up and carry me. I felt peace — God's peace.

From that point on, I'd tell everyone, "We're going to go into that room and Jeff is not going to know he's dying. He's not going to know anything except that we have to make each moment count and be happy every day." I learned that when you're broken, completely broken, and nobody can fix anything, that's when you have to be totally dependent on God.

Jeff died on his sixth birthday. Mike and I had slept in his hospital room for eight days, but I wanted to make Jeff's birthday special. The nurses decided Jeff was going to have the greatest birth-day with little gifts, party hats and even a cake. The best present would be big brother Steve. Even though they were a year apart, they were more like twins, inseparable. Being unable to see each other during Jeff's hospital stays was difficult on both boys. Steve was so excited about finally seeing Jeff.

When I woke up the morning of Jeff's birthday, I heard him say, "I'm dying."

He wasn't upset, but I began to roar at God. *"Not him! Jeff will not die today, God! You will not take him on his birthday!"* I just kept praying this over and over. With everything I had, I threw myself into a tug-of-war with God.

Fortunately, Jeff was not in any pain. My

husband was just kind of numb. He stood at Jeff's feet and I was at his head, just holding him.

At one point, Jeff said, "Mom, I think I'm going to go home now."

I said, "Yes, you're going to get better, and we're going to go home."

Jeff said, "No, I'm going into the jungle, and there's a note. Can you tell me what the note says?"

I'm thinking, *"The note? What note?"*

He asked me again, "Mom, what does that note say?"

Then I said, "The note says, 'Jesus loves you.' Do you love Jesus?"

And Jeff answered, "Oh, yeah."

I whispered, "Jeff, don't be afraid. It will be all right. It's going to be beautiful where you're going, and we're going to come one day to be with you."

I kept saying to God, *"Don't take him on his birthday. Can't You take him on another day?"* But I felt him being pulled away.

Jeff was lifting up his arms, but not for me. He was looking at something over my head and reaching for it with all he had. I knew it was time. Jeff wasn't frightened at all, and suddenly, neither was I.

Chapter Three

A peace had filled the room before the monitors went off and the staff began shouting, "Code Blue!" They got on him and tried to resuscitate him. When they stopped, I literally felt Jeff leave. I know it sounds bizarre, but I felt his spirit pass by us through a window, and I heard Jeff say, "Bye, Mom," real sweetly. That was it. It was over.

When they left us alone with him, the peace of God filled the whole room.

I knew Jeff would get a better birthday party in heaven than I could ever give him, but that didn't make it any easier to tell Steve that there was not going to be any party with us. People think kids don't grieve, but that's not true. My son grieved hard because he didn't get to tell his brother goodbye.

To cope, Steve wrote notes to Jeff. Then he'd fold them up and try to shoot them with his bow and arrow into the air, but they always came back down. One day, Steve shot a note up to Jeff, and it didn't come down. He came running inside, "Oh, Mom, I sent a note to Jeff, and he got it!"

I said, "I know he did. And I know he loves you."

Steve said, "Yep, I know." That was the last note

Steve ever shot.

My grief was made worse by comments from other Christians, such as, "If you had prayed in Jesus' name, Jeff would still be alive."

Or they'd ask, "What kind of sin did you do in your life that made your son sick?"

One family member even said, "You must have done something, or God wouldn't have done this to you." I worried that I had caused Jeff's death. Deep down I knew they were wrong, but I couldn't see the truth. I felt so terribly confused. Still, I knew confusion was not from God.

When it came to religion, I was pretty mixed up. I had gone to Sunday school and church my whole life, and I gave my heart to Jesus as a little girl. Since my parents were different types of Baptists, they disagreed over the path to salvation. I couldn't understand how two people who believed in Jesus could butt heads so much. Then I married a Catholic, which confused me even more. I was so hung up on what different churches taught that I couldn't relax and give my confusion to God.

I didn't want to know about doctrine and denominations. I wanted to know *HIM*. Jesus. I wanted to know Jesus in a way that when I read, prayed and talked to Him, He would show me the truth. I wanted the truth. I didn't want to believe what my mom believed, what my dad believed or what my husband believed. I wanted to know God. I began to call out, *"If You are real, reveal Yourself to me!"* I was on a quest. Even if I had wanted to, I couldn't have run away from God.

As I joined Bible studies, tried lots of churches and researched God's Word, I began to learn about Jesus' beautiful gift of unconditional grace. Because of His death on the cross for us, we are loved regardless of what we do that's good or what we do that's bad. Jeff didn't die because of a church's rule about how I should pray or someone's past sin. I finally knew God doesn't *do* bad things to us. God has no tally sheet of all our rights and wrongs. He didn't *give* Jeff a tumor. We live in fallen world; that's why we have disease, unhappiness and everything else that's wrong here on earth.

Thankfully, I now know we were not created to live on earth forever. This is a waiting place. Jeff is already in heaven laughing, singing and praising God. One day I'll be standing there, in front of

Jesus, with Jeff right by my side.

My quest to grow closer to Christ was far from over. Learning to trust God with my life was one thing. Trusting God with Steve and Marla's lives was another.

The few times I let Steve and Marla get into a car with anybody, I'd constantly pace, thinking, *"What if something happens to them? How could I handle it?"*

When the kids said they were sick, I'd say, "You are not sick."

And they'd say, "Mom, I *am* sick."

"YOU ARE NOT SICK! It's just a cold; you are *not* sick!"

When one of your children dies, it's hard to trust God with the two you have left. I eventually began to see that as much as I loved my kids, God loved them more. Little by little, I started to let go, but God was not done teaching me about Himself through my kids.

Two years after Jeff's death, God sent me back to the same doctor at the same hospital, but with another child. All of my kids were born with heart murmurs, which we were told they would outgrow.

Chapter Three

But during Steve's school physical, his pediatrician heard something wrong with his heart. At the hospital they put Steve through an EKG and a heart test, but the x-ray showed a tumor on Steve's heart. I pleaded, "Don't say that word to me! I can't take it." All I could think was, *"First one son and now this one."*

While waiting a week to see the heart specialist, I asked everyone I knew to pray for Steve. I tried to believe this couldn't happen to me twice, even though I knew it could. I asked everyone to pray for a miracle, so maybe this time would be different. I believed in prayer, in miracles and in Christ's love for Steve. From my faith, I found my hope.

The night before I took Steve to see the heart specialist, I had a dream. Jeff was sitting at the kitchen table, and I yelled, "Jeff! What are you doing here?"

"Well, Mom," he said, "I've been here all the time."

I said, "No, you haven't. You died."

"No, Mom. I didn't. I have never left you." Mike and the kids came in and began to kiss and hug him, but Jeff said, "Stop. I'm here. I've never left you."

We laughed and played with Jeff like he had never left until I started to carry him up to bed.

In my dream, God spoke to me. "You have to give him back to Me now."

I said, "No. I'm not giving him back."

I ran away, holding Jeff tighter, but God said, "Yes, Sharon, you have to give him back." That's when I looked down and saw that the little boy I was carrying wasn't Jeff; it was Steve. I woke up, panicked. This was another tug-of-war with God, only not over Jeff, but Steve.

The next day at the heart specialist, I started getting sick, thinking, *"God, I'm not strong enough to do this. Not again. I can't go through this anymore."*

Finally, the specialist walked in. "Here's our tests; here are the hospital's tests. All of their tests show he had a tumor, and all of our tests show the tumor is gone. We can't understand it. We were out there in the hallway, looking at the tumor on their set of x-rays. But on today's x-rays, his heart is perfectly fine. There has to be some mistake. We have no explanation except to tell you that this child is fine."

Chapter Three

I began to breathe again, "Thank You, God!" I knew God had healed Steve, and all those prayers were answered. We just laughed and cried all the way to the car.

Steve kept saying, "I'm OK, huh?"

And I'd laugh and say, "You're fine!!" It was such a relief, such a relief. God had blessed me beyond compare.

It has been 32 years since Jeff's death, but you never get over losing your child. The death creates a hole, and although God heals the wound, the hole is still there. You learn to live with hurt. When Jeff's kindergarten class graduated from high school, it hurt. When I'd wonder how he would have looked or what his marriage would have been like, it hurt. At more than one point, I thought I would be swallowed up by my grief.

But somehow, with time, God has given me peace. If I'd been asked as a new mom if I could ever feel peace again if my child died, I'd have shouted, "Of course not! I couldn't even live without my children." With time, though, God has given me the sweetest, most unbelievable peace. That's the real miracle.

Now I can laugh at a joke, enjoy being alone or make plans for the future — all things I believed at one time I would never do again. Jeff is still a part of my life, and miraculously, so is the peace that transcends understanding.

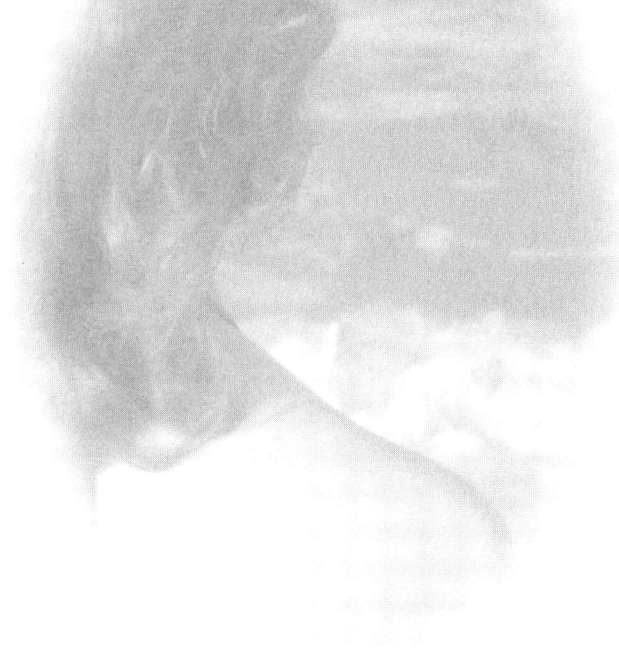

My loving Lord,

Don't
let me *hold back
from You* any
longer.

Help me
to *trust* You in
all things
with an inward certainty.

Thank You

for being the
*Lord God
Almighty*

yesterday, today *&* tomorrow.

I place *all* my *faith* in **You.**

Amen

Trust in what you know about God.

Chapter Four

When Will the Ache Go Away?

He *will* **not** *let
the darkness
and lies*
claim you

Black, Slippery, Nasty Stuff

$\mathcal{P}$erhaps you've come to the place where, although you can't clearly see God's purpose, you trust He's in control and working all things for good. God may feel more like a secret agent in your life than the knight on the white horse that you were hoping for, but you know He's there, busy cleaning up ugly things for the salvation of mankind. In some ways, knowing this helps; there's a layer of struggle that's been removed from your burden, but not the ache. Why is it surprising that grief can be accompanied by a physical ache in your heart?

The ache is part of grieving. Please remember, everyone grieves. Christians do not get to take a pass on living through the stages of grief. Regardless of your devotion, maturity or experience of God, you must grieve, complete with the ache. This ache is not a sign of a lack of faith, only evidence of an absorbing love for the one you have lost.

Some days the ache is a constant companion; other times it's a momentary reminder of your loved one's sweetness. This ache from a lost love can bring tears when an endearing moment is replayed in your mind. Love is a powerfully strong thing that is not intended to go away, ache or no ache. But the ache can have another side that is not so tender. This darker ache often comes from unanswered questions like these:

Was he in pain?
Did she know I loved her?
Why did she die now?
Was he still angry with me?

Chapter Four

Is he in heaven?

What would she want me to do now?

Should I have done more?

The ache from these questions is not poignant or endearing. It is heavy — at times to the point of being crushing.

But answers are coming. When Jesus returns to take us home to heaven, He will make all things new. Jesus will make *you* new. Through your faith in Jesus, you will become perfect in body and soul. With this transformation comes perfect understanding. That's right. You will understand everything. Your list of questions for God will be obsolete because you'll already know the answers. Can you imagine the relief when you completely understand the how's, when's and why's buried in your grief? On that glorious day, this death, and all things, will be put *completely* to rest.

But where is the relief for today? Unanswered questions seep too easily into the sadness of your grief, often accompanied by the dreaded "if only's."

"If only I had taken her to the doctor sooner." "If only I had been driving the car." Not all "if only's" concern death. Perhaps it's even more difficult when they concern life. *"If only I had said, 'I love you,' one more time." "If only I could take my words back." "If only he had come to me for help." "If only I had talked to her about Jesus."* Through your grief, you find ways to place these regrets at the feet of Jesus, knowing He can use even our shortcomings for His good. This leaves you still aching, but intact, knowing you are a treasured child of God.

So one path for your unanswered questions is toward Jesus, the other path leads you to wander in the darkness. Darkness is anything in this world that is not from God. Most people don't drop into darkness; they approach it unknowingly, like a young child who is unaware he has left his mother's side. Grief, or any kind of human suffering, can make a person more susceptible to such frightening wandering.

Let me be clear: I'm not saying that the feelings of

anger and depression required to grieve will lead you into darkness. These stages of grief can be healing. But the "if only's" can dump layers of shame, recrimination, bitterness or apathy on top of your grief, keeping out the light. Then your pain is more than grief for your loss; it is despair for who you are and where your life is leading. Hopelessness is your new companion. Eventually, the darkness becomes so familiar that you don't remember what it felt like to be bathed in light. At this point, you have wandered past grief and into darkness.

Now, a battle has begun. Will the suffering in your life draw you closer to God or farther away? Will the darkness slowly demolish the hope, joy and love in your life? Everything about this battle is horrifying.

In the midst of your emotional battle, thoughts of Jesus as your Rescuer might make you recoil. *"So, where **is** Jesus and **how** can He possibly take away my despair? He didn't stop my loved one from dying; He's not bringing him back from the dead. So what **is** Jesus doing?"* Let me tell you: Jesus is snatching your life from the darkness and replacing it with His light.

We typically think of Jesus as battling for our souls, and He does! Yet once we know Jesus is our Savior, we figure, *"Great! The battle over me is won."* And it is! *Nothing* can separate you from the love of Christ — not death or life or angels or demons or the present or the future or any powers or height or depth or anything else in all creation (Romans 8:38 – 39). But listen. Regardless of the power of the seal of your salvation, Satan still wants to sink his claws into you and rip away your hope. That, my friend, is darkness. The Bible says, "Satan prowls around like a roaring lion, looking for someone to devour" (1 Peter 5:8). Trust that there is no battle Jesus cannot win! But how?

It's time to look at Jesus' battle plan. The first and toughest step to conquering the darkness is seeing it. To find the darkness in your life, look into your thoughts. The darkness sounds different in your mind than the light. Walking in the light brings thoughts of hope, praise and possibility. Walking in the dark brings lies. Lies such as these are Satan's specialty: *"I deserve to be alone." "I don't care." "No one cares." "This pain will never end." "It's all my fault." "It hurts so much I'd rather die."* Do you see how these lies can pull you away from God? It's so tempting to buy into the lies of Satan and forget the promises of God. At one time or another, each of us thinks of lies like these that make God sad. But when the lies feel like truths — that's scary.

As you repeatedly listen to the lies, they impact your life in subtle ways. The temptation is to rarely share these dark thoughts except with people who agree with them. Unfortunately, this fallen world gives us plenty of fuel to support the lies. With time, the lies become comfortable. You may even believe that you need them to go on. *"I just need to accept that everything is hopeless, and then I can move on."* Perhaps you've tried to stop thinking about the lies, only to find yourself more distraught because you can't seem to stop them. This darkness is black, slippery, nasty stuff that's hard to hold on to, and even harder to make go away. It's kind of like a massive oil spill all over the shoreline of your brain.

Picture a giant tanker pumping millions of gallons of oil into the ocean. Like a massive spider, the black sludge spreads over pristine waters and picturesque shorelines and — inevitably — it covers defenseless wildlife. The thought of thousands of beautiful, majestic birds dripping from beak to claw in thick layers of black oil is enough to make you want to cry. Can you imagine looking down a beach, seeing countless birds unable to escape their demise? The vastness of such a disaster is second in size only to the feeling of futility at any attempt to save so much wildlife. Fortunately, the feeling of futility does not stop the rescuers. How do they attack the problem? One bird at a time.

The rescuer finds the oil-drenched bird and begins with supplying sustenance: food and water. After being placed in a plastic tub, the fowl is given a good bath with mild soap and warm water. The rescuer uses a water pick or toothbrush to give special care not to damage the eyes and ears. At this point, the bird's natural instincts kick in and it begins to bathe itself, secreting and rubbing its feathers with oil that acts as a conditioner. When the bird is healthy again, the rescuer releases it back into the wild, hopefully in a cleaner environment. What does the rescuer do next? He picks up another bird and starts the process all over.[1]

In our world, rescuers get overwhelmed, tired and discouraged. Each disaster requires learning the best way to clean it up through trial and error. There's confusion at the scene over the lack of supplies and manpower for the cleanup. And, at some point, the money runs out and the decision is made that the cleanup will end, whether it is completed or not.

Praise God that in Christ we have a Rescuer who always knows what to do, never feels discouraged and, most importantly, *never* stops until He is victorious! Before the first tear on your cheek or ache in your heart, Jesus was with you, ready to battle your

"We have a

personal darkness. He seizes each and every lie and longs for you to smother it in His truth. Just as a bird has to secrete the pure, clean oil to replace the nasty, black sludge, you have to reach out and bathe yourself in God's truth. Jesus doesn't just rip the lies away; He replaces them with His truth. And each time a new lie surfaces or an old one reappears, Jesus restores it to truth again and again and again. That's the way the battle is won.

So the first step in the battle plan is to see the darkness, the lies. The next step is to replace the lies with God's truth found in the Bible. The apostle Paul talks of taking every thought captive and making it obedient to Christ (2 Corinthians 10:5). This is about recognizing the lies, finding God's truth for that lie, and then each time that the lie comes to mind, replacing it with thoughts of truth. Not just once or twice or for a week or two but every time you recognize a lie, replace that thought with God's truth. The problem is you can't abolish lies without truth. Here is one dose of truth:

Rescuer who...

- You do not deserve to be alone — God wants you to be in His presence every moment of your life. *"Never will I leave you; never will I forsake you"* (Hebrews 13:5).

- God more than cares for you — You are His joy, His smile and His laughter. *Jesus…who for the joy set before Him endured the cross* (Hebrews 12:2).

- This despair will end — Jesus wants to wash away your hopelessness each and every day. *May the God of hope fill you with all joy and peace as you trust in Him* (Romans 15:13).

- Nothing is all your fault — No person's actions are bigger than God's purpose. *And we know that in all things God works for the good of those who love Him* (Romans 8:28).

- The greater your hurt, the greater God's victory in your life — No despair is strong enough to conquer truth. *But thanks be to God! He gives us the victory through our Lord Jesus Christ* (1 Corinthians 15:57).

Listen to this beautiful promise from Jesus: "I am

...never stops until

the light of the world. Whoever follows Me will never walk in darkness, but will have the light of life" (John 8:12). Fear not! Jesus is hunting for ways to rescue you from your disaster. The thing about disaster survivors is that they never forget and they always carry the scars. Despite the aches and scars, they learn new ways to soar. Let Jesus wash you in His truth, repeatedly and unceasingly.

[1] "Oil Spills, Saving Animals, Protecting the Seas." "Green Expander: The Guide to a Green Lifestyle." 10 Jan. 2008, 20 Aug 2008.
http://www.greenexpander.com/2008/01/10/oil-spills-saving-animals-protecting-the-seas/

He is victorious!"

"*I am* the **LIGHT** *of the* *world.*

Whoever **follows Me** will never *walk in darkness,* but will have the *light of life."*

John 8:12

A Meeting With Jesus: Laura's Story

It's typical for middle school students to dare one another to do dumb, harmless pranks. At my son's school, someone started a dare that became deadly. Tragically, a group of kids dared one another to commit suicide. 19 students attempted suicide and the 20th was completed. Our son Jayson was the 20th. He had just turned 13. I knew he was having some friend problems, but I had no idea that suicidal thoughts were even on the radarscope. The families of the 19 students who had attempted suicide quietly took their kids out of the school before any other parents found out. But Jayson knew.

At his funeral, a mom told us Jayson saved her daughter's life. The girl had drunk all the bleach in her house, so Jayson took her to a teacher and got help for her. About three months after Jayson's death, a father called to say Jayson had saved his daughter's life when she had taken all the pills in their house. Jayson took her to the principal's office. I can't believe Jayson never told us about these problems, but I think he knew I would have pulled him out of that school.

If you had known Jayson, you'd know he was always helping people and always smiling. He certainly was not a person whom you'd think would even consider taking his own life. Afterward, families would say to us, "If it can happen to you, it can happen to anybody." Counselors call it situational depression — where many negative things happen all at once. If they happened independently, the person would be able to handle it. A person — especially a teenager — can make a decision to take his own life in just a couple of days.

The first sign something was seriously wrong was less than 24 hours before I found Jayson's body. The night before he died, Jayson was just a kid playing shortstop for his baseball team. He made three outs, three innings in a row. After the game, all these dads said he looked like Ozzie Smith diving for the ball. He loved sports. Everything seemed to be fine until we were home and I went out to the mailbox. Jayson's school progress report had an F, a C and a D. *"What is going on?"* was my first thought. Jayson had always been a great student, making A's and B's even in his gifted classes.

Chapter Four

My husband was out of town, so Jayson and I talked. He said, "Please don't make me go to school; they're going to do something mean to me in the hall." Not knowing what was really going on, I thought things would only get worse if he stayed home. I never knew what playing field we were on. I have replayed that day over and over again, wishing I had let Jayson stay home and tried to get him to talk about what was really going on.

I was completely unaware at the time, but the Internet was a key part of the pressure in Jayson's life. Jayson died in 2000, which was the beginning of a drastic change in technology. At that time, even James Bond's cell phone was as big as a book. The Internet was just becoming popular, but no one really understood the darkness of it. There's no question that the Internet played a huge role in how fast things escalated for Jayson.

Although I knew Jayson was using the computer, I had no idea he was being bullied and harassed. Threats to beat Jayson up were only a small part of the problem. Someone sent an e-mail to 150 kids saying Jayson was gay. Jayson was only 12 years old at the time. How is a 12-year-old supposed to handle something like that? Later, I saw an e-mail of Jayson's that showed his anguish. He wrote, "If I fight, it looks like I have something to hide. If I don't fight, it looks like I'm saying it's true."

It's just cruel. We had cruelty when we were growing up, but we didn't have to relive it. On the Internet or somebody's cell phone, lies are so permanent, so vast, and you can't take them back. One push of a button and the lies are all over the world, and there's no one to hold anyone accountable.

The day of his death, all these kids at school were daring Jayson to kill himself. It was sick, just sick. Later that afternoon on Instant Messenger, Jayson finally caved to the dare and told "friends" online he was going to kill himself. It turns out one was his girlfriend. (He had told me earlier that a girl was being really mean to him, but I didn't know she was his girlfriend.) On the computer, as others listened, she said, "You're a wuss and not man enough to do it." Since then, I've learned that going through a breakup is a huge factor for teen-age suicide.

By 8:30 on the morning of his death, I had called

all his teachers and the school counselor because of his progress report. Mostly I got their voice mail, but the teachers I talked to said, "Oh, he's so smart; he can bring his grades up in a week if he wants to." None of them told me, "Oh, that grade drop is huge." Or, "It's the #1 indicator of teenage suicide, and it's going on around here."

At Jayson's funeral, the school counselor said that she didn't answer the phone that day because she was patrolling the girls' bathroom where girls had been slitting their wrists. There were so many people involved in Jayson's life that day who could have made a difference. I can honestly say that if anyone in his family had known what was going on, Jayson could have received help and he would still be here.

What I found at home that day was a nightmare worse than any horror movie. Because we only had one phone line and Jayson was on the computer, the line was busy when I tried to call him from work. Jayson used a gun, and when I walked into the home office, there was horror everywhere.

With Jayson's death, the world stopped. Everything – sleeping, eating, thinking – stopped. I was just so broken. I can't even explain the pain. It hurt so bad; it was physical. People tell me that they love their kids so much that they would just go insane. Don't they think I wanted to go insane? That would have been a whole lot easier. Sometimes I'd pray, *"Please, God, can a truck plow into me so I don't have to deal with this pain anymore?"* or *"Please help me get through the next 15 minutes."*

A really good friend who lived across the street took me to a counselor shortly after the funeral. The counselor told me, "OK, you're going to get up and get dressed every day, but you're going to have to pace yourself. You won't even be able to drive without thinking about him. You're going to think about him more now than you ever did when he was here." And that was so true. Thoughts of Jayson were constant.

The memories of what I saw in the home office haunted me like a movie in my mind, replaying the horror over and over again. The nightmares were so dreadful I didn't want to go to sleep. At times, the horror of that room would hit me when I was awake. There'd be a horrible pain in my chest — like a knife was in my heart —and I'd have problems breathing.

Chapter Four

At times the panic would literally knock me off of my feet.

Something as simple as the color red could trigger it. I couldn't wear red, see red or have it anywhere around me. At times I could barely function.

At one particular session, my counselor walked me through every horror I saw in that room the day Jayson died. She asked me to describe a specific portion of the room, and then she covered each revolting image in prayer. At the end of the session, I was completely drained but hopeful the session had helped. Before I went home, the counselor explained to me that God still speaks to people through dreams, so I should keep a pen and paper by my bed to record any dream.

Two nights later, I had a dream. It began as the horror movie in my mind, as though a camera lens panned the gruesome image of every wall, floor and even the ceiling of the office. Then, suddenly, in my dream, this bright white light washed every corner of the room. At first I thought it must be Jesus or an angel. All I know for sure is God was there, in that pure clean light, making the dark images disappear.

Then God said, "He's OK. He's with me." And for the first time, somewhere deep within me, I knew Jayson was all right.

I asked, "Jayson, are you OK?"

And Jayson answered, "Mom, duh…it's heaven." I knew I was talking to Jayson, because that's exactly what Jayson would say. Then he added, "It's going to be OK. We will all be together again."

That dream was a gift. The morning of the dream, I knew I would see my counselor at church. I could not wait to thank her and share the news. When I saw her, she already knew before I (or anyone) said a word about the dream. She said when she was praying for me that morning, God told her, "I am going to help Laura with the room today."

From the dream, I found a feeling of peace that solidified so many things. Before it, I had thought Jayson was in heaven, but now I knew he was really there with Jesus. I knew with certainty that I would see Jayson again, and that I would meet Jesus. Before the dream, I had felt hopeless, but now I had the hope that eternity is bigger than here.

The amazing part of this is that at the time of

Jayson's death, I would have said I was a Christian, but I didn't have a personal relationship with Christ. Growing up, I went to church every Sunday and even sang in the choir, but I never really understood. After my marriage, I took the kids to church since my husband was agnostic. Jayson's Sunday school teacher told me that Jayson would throw him questions he would have to go research. I knew how his teacher felt! Sometimes Jayson asked me questions, and I'd have more questions for him. Both of us were pulling closer to Christ in our own ways.

A few months before Jayson's death, I decided to try an adult Sunday school class, and I fell in love with it. I remember the teacher saying, "I have Jesus in my life every day." Despite all my years of sitting in the pews, I didn't understand.

Finally, I said, "I just don't get it how someone can ask Jesus into their life. How does that work?" I still had no concept of a personal relationship with Jesus.

After Jayson's death, the people at church just wrapped their arms around us; some were people we'd never even met before. I felt like I saw Jesus through them. They invited me to the Alpha Course at church, which is designed to answer basic questions about God. In all my pain, it was the one weekly event I wanted to attend. The DVDs had so much information on a level I could understand. Parts would make me laugh, and other parts had wonderful analogies to put things in perspective. I ended up going back and helping with the program, getting more out of it each time. Now I know Jesus in a very real way. The truth is: through everything, Jesus wouldn't let me go.

The more I have come to know Jesus, the more healing He has done in my life. Once, I attended a class on the Holy Spirit which offered an opportunity for prayer. I found myself on my knees asking Jesus to forgive me for the things I knew I did and the things I didn't know I did. I kept saying how sorry I was, not just to Jesus, but to Jayson too. Miraculously, by asking Jesus for forgiveness, I finally forgave myself. Healing takes time. There is a part of me still suffering, but I know Jesus is not done with me yet.

God has really used this tragedy to bring my whole family to know Jesus: my husband, my daughter, my parents, my brother's family and even more family and friends. This was only the beginning of Jesus using our shattered lives for His good.

About a year after Jayson's death, a boy who had been in Sunday school with Jayson told his mom that a kid at school was being picked on and harassed. The boy wanted to help but didn't know how. His mom thought of me because she knew that I had been studying and praying about bullying and teen suicides. Nothing about Jayson's death made sense. It was like waking up every morning with this square, trying to fit it in a round hole. It just wouldn't fit. In trying to understand what happened with Jayson, I became very knowledgeable about the risk factors of teen suicide. Harassment can play a significant role.

When she asked me if I would go talk to his class, I didn't know if I could talk without crying. I told her I would pray and think about it. During the next week, three totally different people (one I had never even met before) all gave me the Bible verse: Genesis 50:20. Joseph tells his murderous, kidnapping brothers that "You intended to harm me, but God intended it for good to accomplish what is now being done, the saving of many lives." That's when

I knew I had to help prevent other families from going through this horror and pain.

After that first talk, I handed out a question-naire. On it I asked if one of the students wanted to tell me something. Two kids said, "This may have saved my life."

Another one said, "This may have helped save my friend's life."

That's how *Be A Positive Light* ministry began. It's become my passion. God has just caused it to grow and made it bigger and bigger. People tell me I am so strong, but it's His ministry and not mine. He gives me the strength because many times I just want to collapse after a talk. Through this ministry, I am truly blessed to see how God is using me for His purpose. It's just darkness brought to light. God's using this ministry to change hearts and change lives.

Now I talk to schools, sports teams, scouts and youth groups about Jayson's story and the warning signs of teenage suicide — where to go for help and how to be a friend. Kids need to understand that everything they do can either help someone or hurt someone. There is Truth and there is right and wrong. I say, "If you see that juicy e-mail going around and you wouldn't want your name in the hot box, just stop it. Stop the rumor. Believe that you can make a difference. For that one person, on that one day, you can change everything. You might not ever know how you helped, but you will know that you did the right thing."

During my talks, I read letters that I have received from kids who went to school with Jayson. They say how sorry they are for some of the stuff they did to him. The author of one letter is a girl who has attended a couple of my talks. She just cries and says, "How could I have been so mean to him?"

I've told her, "We've all done things we wish we hadn't. You're doing the only thing you can do now by walking with God and trying to help other kids."

I thought that more kids would tell me more about what happened to Jayson. There's so much that happened that day that we don't know. Now I've accepted that I'm just not going to know in this lifetime. Even though I've "what if-ed" myself like crazy, I know now that I was doing the best I could with what I knew at the time. It could have driven me insane if I hadn't laid all my unanswered questions down at the cross and said, *"Jesus, this is way too big for me. With Your help I want to intentionally be there for my husband, daughter and family. I have to give it to You."*

When I get to heaven, I will understand what God wants me to understand. That will be enough. There is no finish line for my loss here on earth. Jayson is not going to get better from any illness. My son is not away at college to return home to us. I am not going to see him graduate, get married or have children. The ultimate finish line is eternity.

My whole perspective has to be of eternity. Not this life. The wound is so deep in my soul; I will never be the same person. The only way to get through is to not think about the here and now. Therefore, the things I do today need to have eternal significance. If I do things God's way and not my way, they will. To keep this as my focus, I pray this every day:

 Mychal's Prayer[2]
 Lord, take me where You want me to go,
 Let me meet who You want me to meet,

Tell me what You want me to say,
And keep me out of Your way.
Amen.

Nothing compares to the promise we have in Him.
I try to start my day, every day, with that prayer:
It's not what I want, Jesus, but what You want.

There are two things I know with certainty. One
is, ultimately, we will all be together again with
Jayson in heaven. Living here on this earth is the
hard part, but Jesus knows it's not easy.

The other thing I know that's true is, Jesus will
be here with me the whole time, turning each...

...moment of darkness
into
light.

[2] "To Encourage Greater Faith, Hope & Love Through 'The Saint of 9/11'."
"Saint Mychal Judge." 31 Aug. 2008. http://saintmychaljudge.blogspot.com/

Restore me, Jesus,
once again.
Banish the lies in my mind
and *give me a hunger* for
Your truth.

Shine Your glorious

LIGHT
on me
—and through me—
for all to see.

Thank You *for all the*

Victories

You still
have planned for

my life.

*You
are my*

REDEEMER

in **ALL** *things.*

Amen

Let Jesus wash you in His truth!

Taking a closer look at
God is Bigger Than Your Grief:
A BIBLE STUDY

Chapter One: Will I See Them Again?

1. I am enraptured by God's desire to want to live with us forever. In the Garden of Eden, Adam and Eve would have lived forever by eating of the Tree of Life. When sin entered the world, they were banished from the garden so they would no longer eat from the tree (Genesis 3:22–24).

   But that's not the end of the Tree of Life. The Book of Revelation contains a God-given tour of the City of God after Jesus comes to take us all to live with Him in heaven. Look at Revelation 22:1–2 and picture the beautiful landscape of heaven:

   Then the angel showed me the river of the water of life, as clear as crystal, flowing from the throne of God and of the Lamb down the middle of the great street of the city. On each side of the river stood the tree of life, bearing twelve crops of fruit, yielding its fruit every month. And the leaves of the tree are for the healing of the nations.

   - So where is the Tree of Life?
   - When will we eat of the Tree of Life and live forever?
   - What role does Jesus play in us eating of the Tree of Life and having everlasting life?

- Is it tempting to take the gift of salvation and ever-lasting life for granted?

2. The more we read in the Bible about Jesus taking us home with Him, the easier it is to become impatient with our life here on this earth. The apostle Peter called his early Christian friends "strangers in the world" (1 Peter 1:1). This was Peter's way of saying as Christians, we are meant to be one with Christ in His heavenly kingdom, not suffering here on earth. Peter's friends wanted to know when Jesus would come to fulfill His promise. Here is how Peter consoled them:

    "But do not forget this one thing, dear friends: With the Lord a day is like a thousand years, and a thousand years are like a day. The Lord is not slow in keeping his promise, as some understand slowness. He is patient with you, not wanting anyone to perish, but everyone to come to repentance" (2 Peter 3:8–9).

    - What do you believe he means by saying a thousand years are like a day to the Lord?
    - The word "perish" actually means "to be destroyed." If those who do not come to repentance are destroyed, then Peter is not speaking of physical death, but eternal spiritual death. Write the names of three people who do not know Jesus. How do you see the Lord working in their lives to bring them to Him?
    - Take a moment in prayer to ask the Lord how you can reach out to these people.

3. It's very common for believers to think that pastors or "other Christians" have the Holy Spirit, but not them. This is not true. If you believe that Jesus is your savior, you have the Holy Spirit within you.

For we were all baptized by one Spirit into one body (of Christ) — whether Jews or Greeks, slave or free — and we were all given the one Spirit to drink (1 Corinthians 12:13).

- The body of Christ refers to all believers — yesterday, today and tomorrow. From this verse, is the Holy Spirit in you different than the Holy Spirit in your pastor?

The Holy Spirit is hard to grasp. Jesus knew this. Here's how He tried to explain how to recognize the Holy Spirit:

"The wind blows wherever it pleases. You hear its sound, but you cannot tell where it comes from or where it is going. So it is with everyone born of the Spirit" (John 3:8).

Jesus is saying to look in your past to see the impact of the Holy Spirit in your life.

- Can you think of a time God has touched your life?
- How does looking back and seeing evidence of God in your life affect your faith?

Chapter Two: Why Can't I Get On With My Life?

1. So what would you do if Jesus knelt to wash your feet? Two extreme responses come to mind:

    a. "At last I have the comfort I so desperately need! Thank You, Jesus, for caring for me."

    b. "What? I'm not letting You wash my feet! I'm unworthy!"

Read John 13:6 – 8 to see the apostle Peter's response to Jesus washing his feet:

He came to Simon Peter, who said to Him, "Lord, are You going to wash my feet?"

Jesus replied, "You do not realize now what I am doing, but later you will understand."

"No," said Peter, "You shall never wash my feet."

Jesus answered, "Unless I wash you, you have no part with Me."

- What response did Peter give to Jesus when told his Lord would wash his feet?
- Why do you think Peter responded like this?
- What response would you give if Jesus was kneeling before you right now, about to take your foot into His hand?
- What is difficult about letting others take care of us?
- How does letting others care for us work into God's plans?

2. The apostle Paul calls God the "God of all comfort" (2 Corinthians 1:3). I like that a lot. Not some comfort, but *all* comfort. You name it — He can comfort it! But, as Christians, we should give comfort as well as receive it.

    Praise be to the God…of all comfort, who comforts us in

all our troubles, so that we can comfort those in any trouble with the comfort we ourselves have received from God (2 Corinthians 1:3 – 4).

- What are we to do first — give comfort or be comforted?
- What do you think would happen if you reversed the order? Is it tempting? If so, why?
- Can you think of a time you gave comfort first and received comfort later, or perhaps not received it at all?
- How would the outcome have been different if you had sought comfort from Jesus before you gave comfort?

3. Studying about receiving comfort and peace from Jesus may be easier than understanding how. Fortunately, the following verses read much like an instruction book for placing our burdens before Jesus and receiving His wondrous peace.

Do not be anxious about anything, but in everything, by prayer and petition, with thanksgiving, present your requests to God. And the peace of God, which transcends all understanding, will guard your hearts and your minds in Christ Jesus (Philippians 4:6 – 7).

- What are you to *not* do?
- What are the two activities you are supposed to do? P_____ and P_____.
- What should be in you heart as you do this? T_____.
- What do you present to God?

This is the "how to" section. Present *everything* to God through prayers, being thankful for all the Lord has done for you. Then guess what will happen! Look at the next verse.

- Whose peace?
- Can you understand it?
- What will it guard?
- In whose name?

This is not a magical prayer formula, but comfort and peace often come with consistent and persistent prayer. And this is not a guarantee that you will have your prayer answered just the way you want. But this verse does say that prayer will lead you to having peace at times in your life when you are sure peace is impossible. Sweet, inexplicable peace. You can't get better comfort than that. Through steady doses of prayer and Scripture, this peace will protect your aching heart and your anxious mind in the name of our risen Lord, Christ Jesus.

Chapter Three: Why Did You Let Them Die?

1. It is often easier to see everything that is wrong in the world instead of everything that is right. When I am in the midst of my personal chaos, I need reassurance that God is in control. This verse always touches my heart:
   And we know that in all things God works for the good of

those who love Him, who have been called according to His purpose (Romans 8:28).

- What things does God work for good?
- For whose good is He working?

God can take the smallest concern to the largest devastation and use it not simply for His good, but for the good of each believer. All things are working toward God's purpose to bring His lost children back home.

- Take a moment and pray to God, thanking Him for working wrongs into good. Be specific about the wrongs God is turning into good, whether or not you can see them.

2. You know, it's the senselessness of death that can often hurt the most. When you lose a loved one and it doesn't seem fair, we want justice. The society we live in says we deserve justice. But can we see it? As mere humans, can we really see it? Look at this verse to see where justice comes from:

This righteousness from God comes through faith in Jesus Christ to all who believe. There is no difference, for all have sinned and fall short of the glory of God, and are justified freely by His grace through the redemption that came by Christ Jesus (Romans 3:22-24).

- Who has sinned and fallen short?
- By what are we justified freely?

To be justified is to be just or right. The only way for us to be just is through the grace of Jesus Christ, which none of us deserve. So we live with questions concerning things that, through our human eyes, definitely look senseless.

- What types of tragic things are difficult to trust that God can use for good?
- Have you ever seen God use a tragedy for good? If so, how?

3. The day will come when God will judge the world. But right now His mission is to *save* the world. We learned in question #1 that God can use everything, even the ugliness, to accomplish His goal to live with us forever. What we have to do now is trust.

It's hard to trust anyone completely because so many friends and family have broken our trust, whether from little things or big things. The truth is, we should expect to be disappointed because they're human. But God is different.

- Paraphrase this verse:

If we are faithless, He will remain faithful, for He cannot disown Himself (2 Timothy 2:13).

The word "faithful" translates to "pisto" in Greek, which means "worthy of trust." Complete this verse, substituting "worthy of trust" for "faithful."

*If we are **un**worthy of trust, He will remain _____ ___ _____ , for He cannot disown Himself.*

What does this reassurance of God's character mean to you?

Chapter Four: Will the Ache Go Away?

1. I love thinking about the day Jesus returns. What a day that will be! The apostle Paul writes that believers will be changed and have bodies like Christ's. The Greek word for "change" is "allassō", which does not mean "change" as in "change your sheets." It means "to be transformed". How cool is that? Read on as Paul tells how it will happen:

   Listen, I tell you a mystery: We will not all sleep (die), but we will all be changed — in a flash, in the twinkling of an eye, at the last trumpet. For the trumpet will sound, the dead will be raised imperishable, and we will be changed...When the perishable has been clothed with the imperishable, and the mortal with immortality, then the saying that is written will come true: "Death has been swallowed up in victory."

   "Where, O death, is your victory? Where, O death, is your sting" (1 Corinthians 15:51–55)?
   - How fast will you be transformed?
   - What will you be clothed in?
   - Your body will go from being mortal to _____.
   - Then what will come true?

   To be like Christ is to be imperishable, immortal and all-knowing.
   - How does knowing this promise from God impact your view of tomorrow?

2. It's hard to do a Bible study on grieving and not look at

Job. Job was "blameless and upright" (Job 1:1), yet he met unfathomable suffering. His livelihood was taken from him, his children were killed and his health was destroyed. Satan predicted what would happen if Job's pleasant lifestyle turned to suffering. Read Satan's comments to God:

"Does Job fear God for nothing?" Satan replied. "Have you not put a hedge around him and his household and everything he has? You have blessed the work of his hands, so that his flocks and herds are spread throughout the land. But stretch out your hand and strike everything he has, and he will surely curse you to your face" (Job 1:9–11).

- A hedge is a layer of protection. List the things God protected before the disasters in Job's life.
- What had God blessed?
- What does Satan believe will happen if everything is taken away?

This, my friend, is the real battle of darkness vs. light that afflicts suffering Christians. Satan's goal is to use the aftermath of our suffering to tempt us to wander into the darkness and maybe even curse God.

- How do you think Satan tries to accomplish this?
- When you are suffering, grieving or sick, are you more susceptible to pulling away from God?
- How can you do to draw closer to Jesus and resist the temptation?

3. The Bible has a lot to say about our minds. Jesus said

the greatest commandment is to *"love the Lord your God with all your heart and with all your soul and with all your mind"* (Matthew 22:37). Did you catch that? We can love God with our mind! Read Romans 12:2 to learn more:

Do not conform any longer to the pattern of this world, but be transformed by the renewing of your mind. Then you will be able to test and approve what God's will is — His good, pleasing and perfect will.

- To what are you not to conform?
- What will transform you?
- What will you then be able to test and approve?

Acting out our faith can be difficult if we are thinking of the "patterns of this world."

- Is there an area of your thought life that is more susceptible to dark thoughts than others?
- What truths can you think of that could replace these dark thoughts?

All references to the meaning of specific words come from
http://blueletterbible.org/

Continue your experience with

God is Bigger Than Your Grief

at our Web site:

www.Godisbiggerthan.com

- Read "The Rest of the Stories": Brian, Kate, Sharon and Laura tell you where they and their families are in their walks with God.

- See photos of them and leave messages for them.

- Share how you feel about the book with other readers.

- Communicate with the author, Karen Tripp, M.S., and learn of her speaking engagements and book signings.

- Request a book club conference call with the author.

- Buy more copies of *God is Bigger Than Your Grief* and other books in the *God is Bigger*™ series.